Football School

Name: ....

Class: ....

Coaches: ....

Kickito Ergo Sum

To DJ and LB – A.B.
To ABC, with love – B.L.
For Nod, our family Puzzle Champion – S.G.

First published 2020 by Walker Books Ltd
87 Vauxhall Walk, London SE11 5HJ

2 4 6 8 10 9 7 5 3 1

This book has been typeset in Gill Sans MT

Printed and bound by CPI Group (UK) Ltd, Croydon CR0 4YY

British Library Cataloguing in Publication Data:
a catalogue record for this book is available from the British Library

ISBN 978-1-4063-8664-6

WALKER
BOOKS

FSC
www.fsc.org
MIX
Paper from
responsible sources
FSC® C020471

www.walker.co.uk

www.footballschool.co

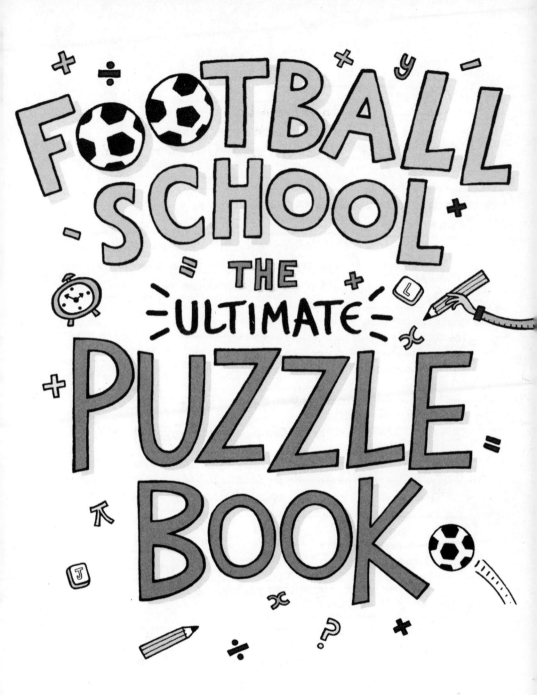

FOOTBALL SCHOOL
THE ULTIMATE
PUZZLE
BOOK

Alex Bellos & Ben Lyttleton

Illustrated by Spike Gerrell

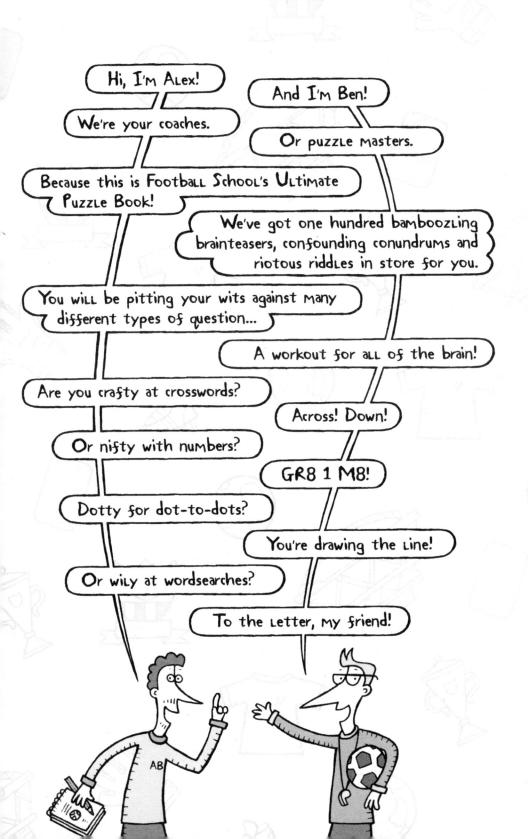

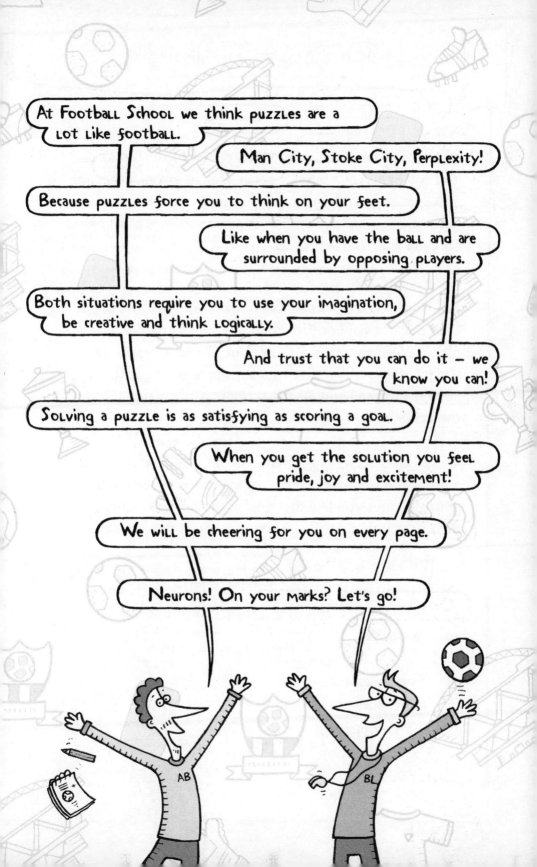

GETTING STARTED

WHAT YOU NEED

All you need is your brain. And a pencil. No, rub that out!
You will need your brain, a pencil and an eraser. Everyone
makes mistakes when solving puzzles – that includes your
parents, Alex and even the best puzzle-solvers of all time.
So keep your rubber handy.

HOW THIS BOOK WORKS

We want you to write in this book. We've made it bigger
than our normal Football School books so that you have
plenty of space to work things out. Often it is only by
writing things down that you can see how to get the
answer. Let the hand do the scribbling as the mind does
the dribbling!

The puzzles aren't organised in order of difficulty. You can
start at the beginning and progress to the end, or start
with the ones you like the look of the best. Whichever
puzzles you do first, check out our handy tips opposite.

TYPES OF PUZZLE

We have sorted the puzzles into five types, each marked
by a symbol at the top of the page. Which one will be
your favourite?

- Visual puzzles
- Word puzzles
- Number puzzles
- Logic puzzles
- Riddles

ALEX AND BEN'S T.I.P.S.
(TERRIFIC INFORMATION FOR PUZZLE SOLVERS)

1. Read the question carefully. Make sure you understand what you are being asked to do.

2. Different puzzles require different methods of solving. For example, some puzzles, especially the number ones, need a step-by-step process to reach the answer. But other puzzles, like the visual ones, are often solved with a simple flash of insight. You may be staring at the page for ages and then suddenly get it. When that happens, it's the best feeling!

3. Riddles are puzzles that are trying to trick you. So read these ones very carefully and question every element. Don't take anything for granted.

4. If you can't do a puzzle, try not to look at the answers. Come back to it later. Your brain will carry on trying to solve the puzzle while you get on with the rest of your day. When you return to the problem, you might have a fresh idea, or see the image in a different way. You'll be amazed by what you can do!

The Preston North End mascot is called Deepdale Duck.
Here's a duck. What other animal can you spot?

The answer is: ....

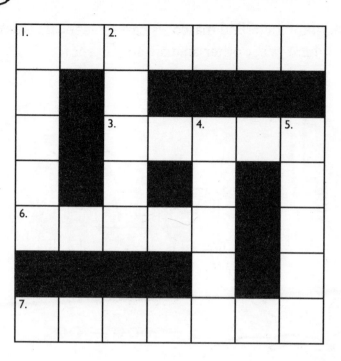

Across:

1. Merseyside club (7)
3. A hat-trick is three of them (5)
6. .... Alexander-Arnold (5)
7. Gunners (7)

Down:

1. Mo Salah's national team (5)
2. Mascot of Crystal Palace, Benfica, Lazio and Eintracht Frankfurt (5)
4. .... Villa (5)
5. Bone in head (5)

3. THE HIDDEN LINK

Can you discover what links these four images?

a)

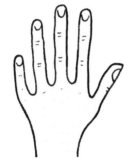

b)

c)

d)

The answer is: ....

Julia and Victoria Principato are two Americans who play for their college football team. They were born to the same parents on the same day in the same year, but they are not twins. How is this possible?

The answer is: ....

....

5. FOR THE WIN

A word ladder begins with two words, one at the top of the ladder and one at the bottom of the ladder. Your task is to find a new word to put in each empty step, such that each new word has only a single letter changed from the word above or below it.

For example, here is how you get from THE to WIN:

T H E
T I E
T I N
W I N

Can you fill in the following two ladders?

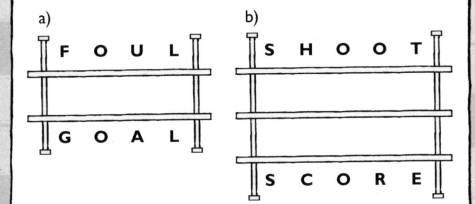

a)

F O U L

G O A L

b)

S H O O T

S C O R E

Tip: at each step, think of all the possible words you can make by changing a single letter. There may be more than one. If you get stuck with one word, rub it out and try another.

6. COUNTING KIT

Can you work out the numerical value of each symbol? The number at the end of each row or column is the sum of the values in that row or column.

				12
				16
				12
				15
12	18	10	15	

 is number........   is number........

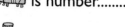 is number........   is number........

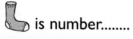 is number........   is number........

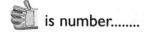 is number........

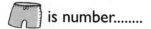

13

7. HEADLINE HORROR

Can you guess the missing words in these headlines?

THE F⚽⚽TBALL TIMES
July 2020

Striker nets hat- ███

a) The answer is ....

THE F⚽⚽TBALL TIMES
July 2020

Star in ███ -record transfer bid

b) The answer is ....

THE F⚽⚽TBALL TIMES
July 2020

Under ██ beats Utd in FA Cup shock

c) The answer is ....

THE F⚽⚽TBALL TIMES
July 2020

My penalty ██-█ nightmare

d) The answer is ....

When two football teams play each other in a league, the winning team gets 3 points and the losing team gets 0 points. If they draw, they get 1 point each. At the end of a competition between Argentina, Brazil and Peru, the table looked like this. Can you fill in the scoreboards below?

	Matches played	Goals scored	Goals conceded	Points
Brazil	2	3	1	6
Peru	2	2	2	3
Argentina	2	0	2	0

Brazil v. Peru	
Brazil	☐
Peru	☐

Peru v. Argentina	
Peru	☐
Argentina	☐

Brazil v. Argentina	
Brazil	☐
Argentina	☐

Tip: goals conceded means the number of goals let in.

Can you name all of these ten body parts that are written with words of three letters?

* No, this is not **BUM!** Don't be so cheeky!

Below are five boot laces, each in a tangle. Your task is to work out which ones will make a knot when you pull either end of the lace. Tick the ones that do, and put a cross by the ones that don't. If you can't do it in your head, try them out with a piece of string.

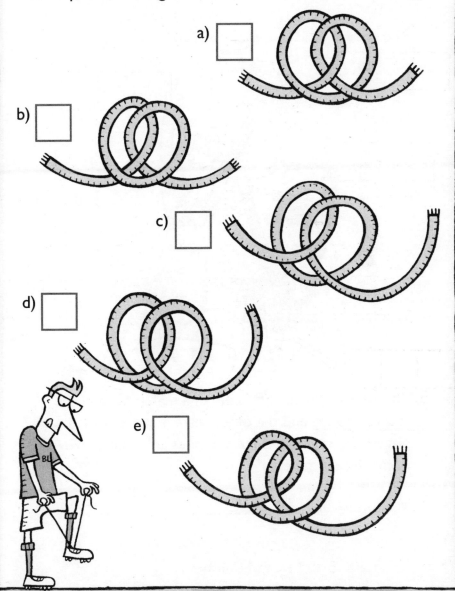

a)

b)

c)

d)

e)

a) A father and son are sitting in a stadium together, having a conversation about the game. All of a sudden, they both stand up and put their hands high in the air. But no goal has been scored. They sit down again and carry on their conversation. What is going on?

The answer is: ....

b) The whistle blows at the end of a match. One of the teams is happy and the other team is sad. But the happy players are crying and the sad ones are smiling. Why might this be the case?

The answer is: ....

A patch of grass is marked with a 5x5 grid, and a ball is placed in the top left cell. The first picture shows a path for the ball that goes through every cell in the grid, travelling only horizontally or vertically between cells, and never crossing itself.

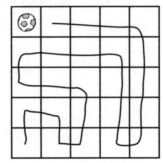

Can you find a similar path where the ball starts in each of the three positions below? Each path must start at the ball, go through every cell in the grid, travel only horizontally or vertically between cells, and not cross itself. (Moving diagonally from one cell to another is not allowed.)

a)

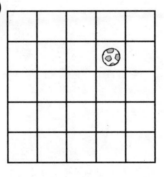

b)

c)

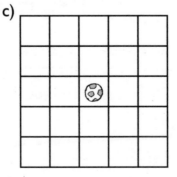

13. BALL COUNT

When the Tottenham Under-16s team won the Youth League, they were surprised to find their trophy was filled with footballs! Can you count how many?

The answer is: ....

14. THE TOP FIVE

Here are five true statements about the top five positions in the league:

United were fourth.
Rovers were in the top two.
City's position in the ranking was an odd number.
Town were not champions.
Albion did better than City but not as well as Town.

Which team was in which position?

Position	Team
1.	
2.	
3.	
4.	
5.	

15. RECTANGLE RIDDLE

Gary the groundsman has painted two rectangles on the grass, as below. The one on the left is 5m wide, and has an area of 30m^2 and the one on the right has an area of 42m^2. Can you work out the width, marked with a ?, of the rectangle on the right?

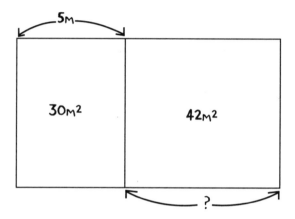

This question is about multiplication. All you need to know is that the area of a rectangle is equal to its height multiplied by its width. You can get the answer without getting out a ruler, just by working out a couple of sums.

The answer is: ....

Tip: start by calculating the length of the left side of the left rectangle.

16. MISSING CLUBS

Can you find the English and Welsh clubs marked below in the grid?

S	Y	B	R	E	D	S	W	A	N	S	E	A
O	T	P	O	R	T	S	M	O	U	T	H	A
U	I	O	P	U	U	S	W	E	R	L	C	R
T	C	Y	K	R	R	L	R	B	R	E	H	S
H	L	C	N	E	E	N	U	U	A	E	E	E
A	O	O	O	A	T	S	E	T	P	D	L	N
M	T	B	Q	V	S	V	T	M	O	S	S	A
P	S	O	P	E	E	V	M	O	O	N	E	L
T	I	L	R	R	H	N	E	S	N	U	A	L
O	R	T	T	H	C	C	T	P	L	N	T	U
N	B	O	L	I	N	T	C	R	E	W	E	H
O	N	N	C	R	A	W	L	E	Y	T	I	C
S	N	O	D	K	M	F	F	I	D	R	A	C

Arsenal	Coventry	Leeds	QPR
Bolton	Crawley	Luton	Southampton
Bournemouth	Crewe	Manchester Utd	Spurs
Bristol City	Derby	MK Dons	Stoke
Cardiff	Everton	Portsmouth	Swansea
Chelsea	Hull	Preston NE	WBA

Once you have crossed out all these teams, you will have 23 letters remaining in the grid. Can you rearrange these letters to make two other well-known teams?

The answer is: ....

23

17. PATTERN POSER

Look at the patterns on these five football kits and work out whether kit a), b) or c) comes next.

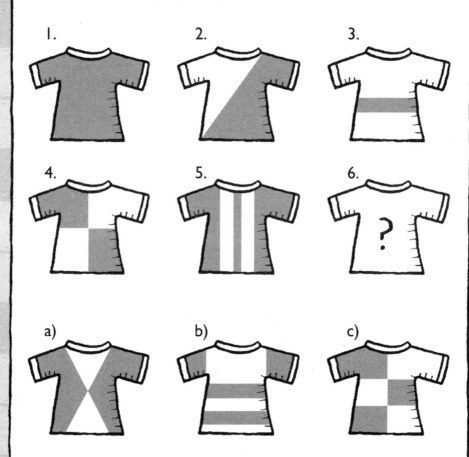

1.

2.

3.

4.

5.

6.
?

a)

b)

c)

The answer is: ....

a) After a thrilling victory, Rovers jump ahead of the second-place team in the league table. What position in the table are Rovers now in?

The answer is: ....

b) After a hard-fought victory, Wanderers edge past the bottom club in the table. What position are they now in?

The answer is: ....

In the first picture there are six fans. But when the sections marked 1. and 2. are rearranged, as shown in the second picture, there are only five fans. Where has the missing fan gone?

The answer is: ....

This jigsaw puzzle is missing the last piece. Can you find the right piece to complete the puzzle?

a)

b)

c)

d)

The answer is: ....

Match the pairs. Which one is the odd one out?
There's also three of one object. Can you spot it?

Can you discover the Star Players whose names have been muddled in these anagrams? An anagram is when you rearrange the letters to make a new word or phrase.

a) I O P E N M A N A G E R

Clue: USA

The answer is: ....

b) C O R D I A L S T A R O N I O N

Clue: Portugal

The answer is: ....

c) S L I M E I N S O L E

Clue: Argentina

The answer is: ....

d) T H E A L G E B R A

Clue: Wales

The answer is: ....

a) The England team are travelling abroad. They are all in a plane. Directly in front of the plane is a huge mountain range. The pilot does not change her course, speed or altitude. Yet the plane doesn't crash. How come?

The answer is: ....

....

b) One summer afternoon, football fan Lars went to see his local team Tromsø IL, who play in the Norwegian first division. As soon as he walked into the stadium, the police closed the exits because of a security alert. Lars was forced to remain in the stadium for one whole week! Yet he still managed to get home before the sun went down. How come?

The answer is: ....

....

A rectangle the shape of a football pitch is marked up with grid lines, as shown in the examples below. The most obvious way to cut the rectangle into a left half and a right half is to draw a straight line down the middle, like on a football pitch. But we can also draw a zigzag line down the middle, as shown on the right. This line also divides the rectangle into two identical halves, because if you were to cut out each half, you would find that you can place them perfectly on top of each other.

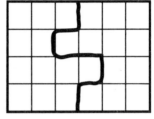

Find two other ways to cut the rectangle into identical right and left halves, and draw them on a) and b) below. In each case the dividing line must include the thick black line marked, and only follow the lines of the grid.

a)

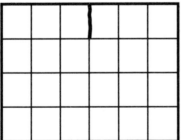

b)

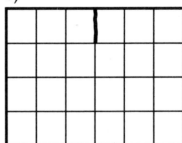

In the following eight sentences, we've stolen the letters of some of the words, leaving only the first letter behind. Can you work out the original words to complete the sentences? We've done the first one for you.

a) A F T has 11 P
A Football Team has 11 Players

b) A Y has 12 M
....

c) A M lasts for 90 M
....

d) A H has 5 F
....

e) The P L has 20 C
....

f) A D has 24 H
....

g) E have won 1 W C
....

h) If you score 3 G, it's a H-T
....

Tip: some sentences are about football, but some are not.

26. NUMBERLINK

Can you link each pair of numbers with a line?
Each line must stay in the grid; it can only pass up or
down, left or right, but not diagonally; it must not go
through another number; and lines cannot cross each
other. Each little square can only have one line.

Here is an example:

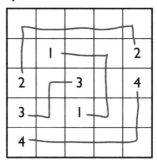

Tip: use a pencil,
and have a rubber at
hand. It's easy to
make mistakes!

1					2
		1			
	2			4	
3					
4					3

27. THE THREE PEGS

Three pegs are in a row on the changing-room wall. On each peg hangs a shirt. Each shirt displays a player's name and a squad number. Underneath each shirt is that player's boots. The players are Smith, Jones and Robinson, the numbers are 3, 5 and 7 and the boots are orange, pink and white, but not necessarily in that order.

Read the following four statements. Can you use them to work out the correct positioning of the names, numbers and colours? Write them in the spaces below.

Jones' shirt is to the left of the pink boots.
The player to the right of the number 7 shirt has orange boots.
Smith's shirt is in the middle.
The number 3 shirt is on the leftmost peg.

	Left peg	Middle peg	Right peg
Player name:	....	....	....
Squad number:	....	....	....
Boot colour:	....	....	....

35

The Leicester City mascot is called Filbert Fox.
Here are two foxes lying down on their sides.
By drawing only four lines, can you turn the picture
into a picture of two foxes running?

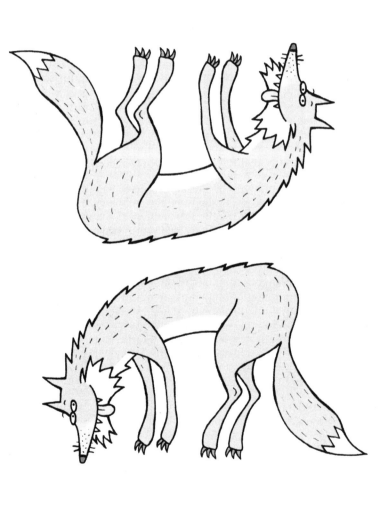

The match kicks off at 4.10 p.m. Can you draw the hands on the clock to show when half-time starts?

Tip: a football match is 90 minutes long.

This high-scoring game conceals a vegetable.
Can you unpeel the puzzle to discover what it is?

ROVERS V. UNITED

20–20

The answer is: ....

Here are the names of eight countries that have won the World Cup with the consonants taken out. Fill in the gaps to work out which countries they are. We've done one for you.

a) | S | P | A | I | N |

b) | U | | U | | U | A | |

c) | | E | | | A | | |

d) | E | | | | A | | |

e) | | | A | | I | |

f) | | | A | | | E | |

Tip: consonants are the letters in the alphabet which aren't vowels.

g) | A | | | E | | | I | | A |

h) | I | | A | | |

39

32. TANTRUM TEASER

Can you find anagrams of the following phrases? An anagram is when you rearrange the letters to make a new word or phrase. Here the anagrams are all English football clubs.

a)

THE UNARMED INSECT

The answer is: ....

b)

WHAT GIANT LICE

The answer is: ....

c)

OH THE TOP TANTRUMS

The answer is: ....

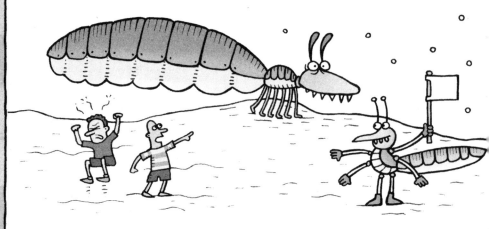

d)

V I T A L L O A N S

The answer is: ....

e)

S T O C K Y T I E

The answer is: ....

f)

E L E C T R I C Y E T I S

The answer is: ....

The day after the match is five days before the day after tomorrow. If today is Saturday, what day was the match on? Use the days of the week below to help you work it out.

M	T	W	Th	F	Sa	Su

The answer is: ....

Start at the dot marked 130 and join it to the dot marked with a number that is 7 less than 130, and then to the dot marked 7 less than that. Continue joining dots marked 7 less than the previous dot until you can carry on no further. You'll feel like a champion if you get it right!

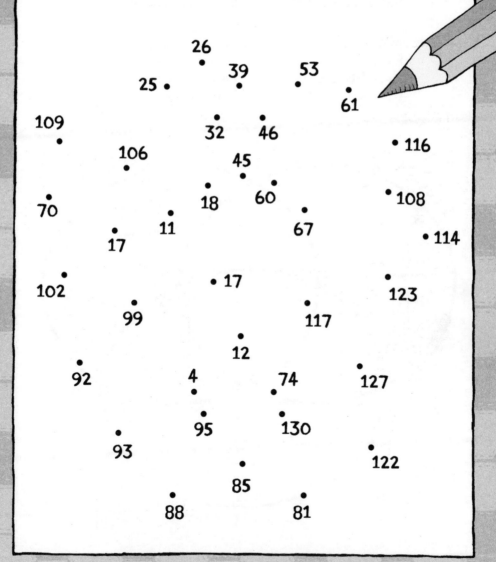

26

25

39

53

61

109

32

46

106

45

116

70

18

60

108

11

67

114

17

102

17

123

99

117

12

92

4

74

127

95

130

93

122

85

88

81

43

In a Venn diagram, each circle describes a property. For example, in the Venn diagram below Lionel Messi is inside the circle labelled "Is a striker", but is outside the circles labelled "Surname begins with S" and "Is British". That's because Messi is a striker, but is not British and his name does not begin with an S. Can you correctly place the other six footballers in the other six regions?

Harry Kane
Harry Maguire
Mo Salah

Bernardo Silva
Raheem Sterling
John Stones

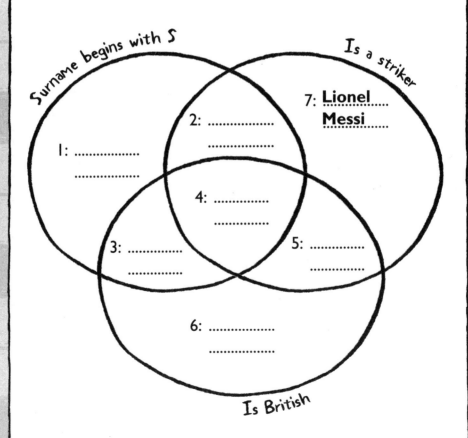

Can you discover what links these four images? It might help to say aloud what you see in each image.

a)

b)

c)

d)

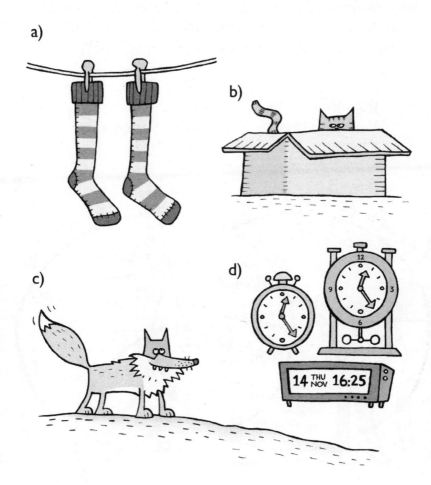

The answer is: ....

Chelsea bought two players for £110 million. One of the players cost £100 million more than the other. How much did each of them cost?

The answer is: ....

38. BETWEEN THE LINES

This criss-cross pattern conceals two teams. Can you work out which ones?

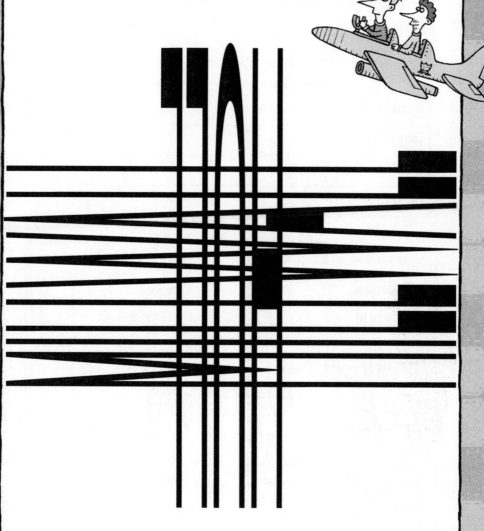

The answer is: ....

39. TABLE TEASER

The home nations played in a competition and this was the final table. They each played each other once. Can you work out what all the scores were in each of the matches?

	Matches played	Goals scored	Goals conceded	Points
Scotland	3	7	0	9
England	3	3	2	6
Wales	3	1	6	3
N. Ireland	3	0	3	0

Scotland v. England

Scotland ☐
England ☐

Wales v. N. Ireland

Wales ☐
N. Ireland ☐

England v. N. Ireland

England ☐
N. Ireland ☐

Scotland v. Wales

Scotland ☐
Wales ☐

N. Ireland v. Scotland

N. Ireland ☐
Scotland ☐

Wales v. England

Wales ☐
England ☐

Tip: if you've forgotten how points work see Puzzle 8.

48

A₁

Fill in the following word ladders:

a)
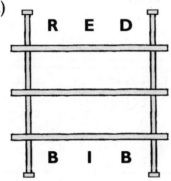
R E D

B I B

b)
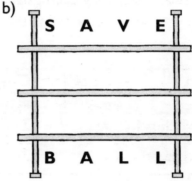
S A V E

B A L L

For these word ladders, we've given you an extra clue:

c)
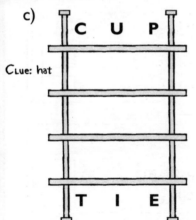
C U P

Clue: hat

T I E

d)
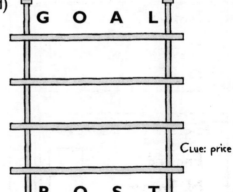
G O A L

Clue: price

P O S T

Tip: see Puzzle 5 for word ladder rules.

Can you spot at least 50 things starting with the letter B?
Write a list on a piece of paper.

Can you link each mascot to their correct shadow?

The coach, the assistant coach, the goalkeeping coach and the physio are sitting on the bench.

The assistant coach is to the left of the coach.
The physio is to the right of the goalkeeping coach.
The assistant coach is to the right of the physio.

Who is sitting where?

The answer is: ....

44. ARITHMETIC NUMBER

Each of the numbers from 1 to 10 is represented by a different symbol. Can you work out which number is which symbol from the equations below?

⚽ x ⚽ = 👟

⚽ x ⚽ x ⚽ = 👕

⚽ x 🚩 = ⚽

⚽ x 🟨 = 📖

⚽ + 👟 = 📖

⚽ x 🧦 = 🧴

🟨 x 🟨 = 🥅

⚽ is number........   📖 is number........

👟 is number........   🥅 is number........

🧴 is number........   🧤 is number........

🟨 is number........   🧦 is number........

🚩 is number........   👕 is number........

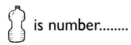

54

45. MIRROR MIRROR

Read the ten words below. If you turn the page upside down and read it in a mirror, only one of the words below will appear exactly the same. Can you work out which one? Try it to find out!

BOX	**SPOT**
DUG-OUT	**BENCH**
BAR	**POST**
LINE	**TURF**
CIRCLE	**GOAL**

The answer is: ....

The Premier League ball is based on the dodecahedron, a shape made from 12 pentagons.

One way to make a physical model of a dodecahedron is to cut along the edges of the 12 connected pentagons below, and fold along the joins.

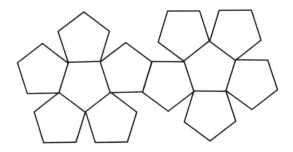

In this puzzle, however, no cutting is required. The challenge is to draw the image of the 12 pentagons in such a way that you never move your pencil off the page and you never go over the same line twice. Can you do it?

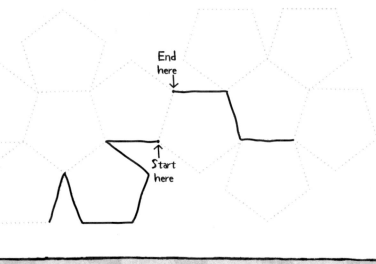

End here ↓

↑ Start here

47. IN POSITION

City's defensive line consists of Amber, Beth and Christie. The girls are standing with one on the left, one in the middle and one on the right. Amber is to the left of Beth, and Christie is to the right of Amber.

This information is not enough to determine with 100 per cent certainty which girl is in which position. However, we can still deduce some facts about them. For example, which of the following five statements must be true?

a) Beth is furthest to the left.
b) Christie is furthest to the right.
c) Amber is in the middle.
d) Amber is furthest to the left.
e) None of the above statements.

The answer is: ....

Emma is coaching her school team and wants to keep the tactics secret. So she writes them on a piece of paper using a code. Her code is what's known as a Caesar cipher, which is when each letter is substituted by a letter a fixed number of places (a shift) along the alphabet. Her cipher has a shift of 7, which means that A becomes H, B becomes I, C becomes J, and so on.

Emma has turned her message into the following code:

VBY VWWVULUAZ HYL H
NVVK ALHT IBA DL JHU
ILHA AOLT PM DL JYVDK
AOL NVHSRLLWLY HA
JVYULYZ ILJHBZL OL
PZ UVA JVUMPKLUA HA
OPNO IHSSZ HUK PM DL
WSHF AOL IHSS KVDU
AOL ZPKL VM AOL SLMA
IHJR HZ ZOL PZ ZSVDLY
AOHU VBY DPUNLY

Can you work out the message? For each letter in the code, you need to count back 7 places (the shift) along the alphabet to find the real letter in the message. Let's work out the first word together using the alphabet below:

Y = R

A B C D E F G H I J K L M N O P Q R S T U V W X Y Z A B C

V = O   B = U

So, now we know that **VBY** = **OUR** and we can fill the first word in below. Using the shift and the alphabet, can you work out the rest of Emma's message?

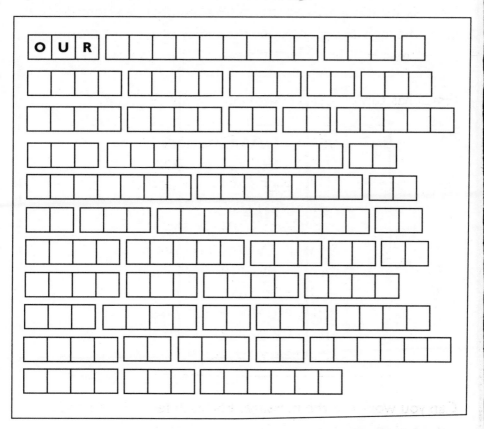

| O | U | R |

49. WHITE LINES

Gary the groundsman has again painted rectangles on the grass. Without measuring, can you work out the area marked with a question mark?

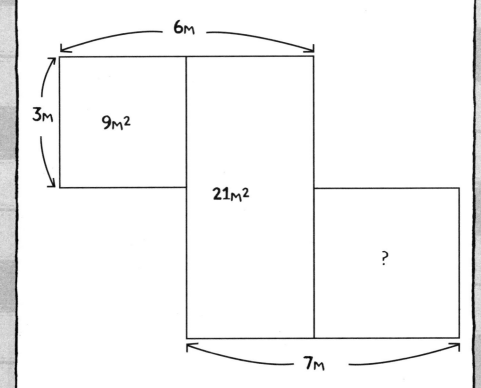

The answer is: ....

Tip: if you've forgotten how to work out the area, see Puzzle 15.

50. WHIFFY WORDS

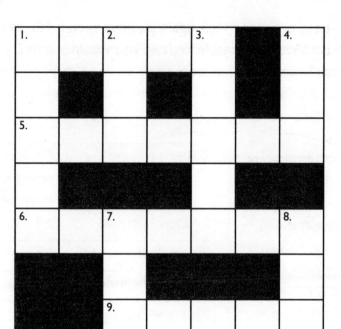

Across:
1. .... and pains (5)
5. Team from Glasgow, or Queen's Park (7)
6. National stadium (7)
9. Tottenham nickname (5)

Down:
1. Bow and .... (5)
2. Lays eggs (3)
3. Pong, whiff, aroma (5)
4. Farts (3)
7. Mr and .... (3)
8. Opposite of no (3)

The world is divided into different time zones. For example, when it is noon in the UK, it is 1 p.m. in France and 2 p.m. in Greece. Time zones are necessary because each country sees the sun rise and fall at different times depending on where they are located.

Using the time-zone chart, you can see that when it is noon in London it will be 8 p.m. in Tokyo, because noon + 8 hours is 8 p.m., and it will be 8 a.m. in Rio de Janeiro, since noon − 4 hours is 8 a.m.

City	Difference from UK in hours
Sydney, Australia	+9
Tokyo, Japan	+8
New Delhi, India	+4.5
Moscow, Russia	+2
Rio de Janeiro, Brazil	−4
Los Angeles, USA	−8

For each of the following games, the host city and kick-off time are stated. Can you calculate what time the match starts if you are watching on TV from the other city marked?

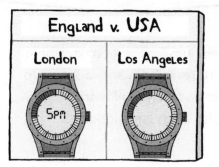

England v. USA

London	Los Angeles
5pm	

Brazil v. Australia

Rio de Janeiro	Sydney
3pm	

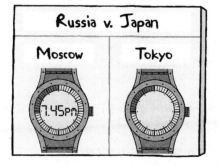

Russia v. Japan

Moscow	Tokyo
7.45pm	

USA v. India

Los Angeles	New Delhi
3.15pm	

India v. England

New Delhi	Manchester
12pm	

52. SARNIE STUMPER

Three football fans, Mo, Jo and Flo, are having a picnic in the park. They each support a different team and their sandwiches have different fillings. Using the following statements, can you work out who each fan supports and what they are eating?

The Celtic fan is eating chicken.
Mo is vegetarian.
Flo has the cucumber sandwich.
The cheese-sandwich eater is no fan of Everton.

You will be able to find the answer by filling in the table below. We've started it for you. From the third statement we know that Flo has the cucumber sandwich, so we tick the Flo/cucumber box. We can also cross off the sandwiches we know she is not eating, and we can cross off the cucumber sandwich option for the other fans. Can you finish the puzzle?

	Celtic	Swansea	Everton	Chicken	Cucumber	Cheese
Mo					x	
Jo					x	
Flo				x	✓	x

53. FOOTBALL SCRABBLE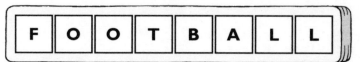

How many words can you make using **only** these letters:

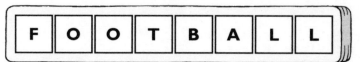

| F | O | O | T | B | A | L | L |

Fill in the boxes with as many other words as you can.
We've done some to get you started.

a) Two-letter words:

| A | T |

b) Three-letter words:

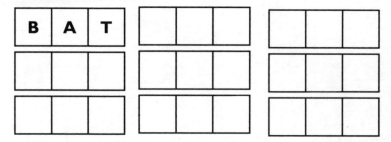

| B | A | T |

c) Four-letter words:

| B | A | L | L |

Tip: there are more two, three, four and five letter-words to be found if you want to carry on playing the scrabble game.

d) Five-letter words:

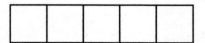

54. SPOT THE DIFFERENCE

Can you spot the 15 differences between these two pictures?

55. WETT AFFAIR

During a training day at the aquatics centre, striker Winnie Wett was holding a bucket full of water. When she turned the bucket slowly upside down, it stayed full of water. It was a normal bucket, with no lid, and the water was not frozen. How did she do it?

The answer is: ....

The trophy cabinet has a three-digit combination lock. To open the lock, you need to place three different digits, between 0 and 9, in the correct positions. Using the following clues, can you work out the correct combination?

3	4	6

No digits are correct.

7	0	4

No digits are correct.

6	9	0

One digit is correct, but in the wrong place.

9	3	1

Two digits are correct, but only one is in the correct place.

5	8	9

One digit is correct, but in the wrong place.

The answer is:

57. DATA CORNER

Here are the stats for 10 players in a pre-season tournament. Use the table to answer the five questions on the opposite page.

Player	Games played	Total mins played	Goals
Timmy Twinkletoes	4	360	6
Oleg O'Legge	4	270	5
Sam Speed	2	180	4
Matt Marvel	4	300	3
Lucky Stryker	4	360	2
Nate Nett	4	250	2
Darren Dribble	4	200	1
Algernon Targett	4	300	1
Brad Spitt	4	10	1
Beau Peep-Peep	4	360	0

Tip: you might need to use a calculator for this puzzle.

a) Which players played every minute of every game?

The answer is: ....

b) Which player is most likely a goalkeeper?

The answer is: ....

c) Which player averaged the most goals per match?

The answer is: ....

d) Which player averaged the most goals per minute?

The answer is: ....

58. SPOT THE DIFFERENCE

Can you spot the 15 differences between these two images?

Can you link each pair of numbers with a line?

Here is an example:

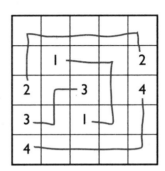

Tip: see Puzzle 26 if you need a reminder on how numberlinks work.

			2		3
	1				4
		2	1		
		5	3		
	4				
					5

60. TABLE TEASER

The final table of a Champions League group stage is shown below. Can you work out what the scores were in each of the matches? We've filled in the first game for you.

	Matches played	Goals scored	Goals conceded	Points
Bayern Munich	3	7	1	9
Juventus	3	3	2	4
Barcelona	3	2	3	4
PSG	3	0	6	0

Bayern v. Barcelona

Bayern	3
Barcelona	0

PSG v. Juventus

PSG	
Juventus	

Bayern v. Juventus

Bayern	
Juventus	

Barcelona v. PSG

Barcelona	
PSG	

PSG v. Bayern

PSG	
Bayern	

Juventus v. Barcelona

Juventus	
Barcelona	

Tip: if you've forgotten how points work, see Puzzle 8.

61. DECIPHER YOURSELF!

Alex left the following message for Spike using a Caesar cipher. But he forgot to tell Spike the shift number!
Can you work out what the message says?

Tip: see Puzzle 48 for the rules.

> GRQ'W WHOO EHQ EXW
> L KLG WKH FDNH LQ WKH
> OLEUDUB. L'OO PHHW BRX
> WKHUH DV VRRQ DV WKH
> JDPH VWDUWV.

To help you figure out the shift, use the alphabet and this clue: the most common letter in the original message is "E".

A B C D E F G H I J K L M N O P Q R S T U V W X Y Z

Once you've worked out the shift, can you figure out the rest of Alex's message?

62. SILLY SENTENCES

We've hidden a European football club in each of the following sentences. Can you spot them all? We've done the first one for you.

a) The sala**mi lan**ded on the floor.

   The answer is: ....**Milan**..........................

b) Nicki Minaj axed her lawyer.

   The answer is: ....

c) The plan to kidnap Olive failed.

   The answer is: ....

d) To wake up, or to stay in bed?

   The answer is: ....

e) Alex had a real, mad, ridiculous, silly and crazy idea.

   The answer is: ....

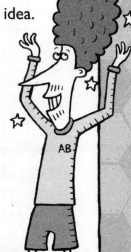

Morse code is a way of encoding the letters of the alphabet with a combination of dots and dashes. Here's the Morse alphabet with balls for the dots and boots for the dashes.

At the end of a day's training, Alex was fed up and decided to write a message in Morse code on the pitch using a ball for a dot and a boot for a dash. Can you read what he is saying? We've done the first word for you.

⚽👟👟 ⚽⚽⚽⚽ 👟⚽👟👟

W..........**H**.............**Y**..........

⚽⚽ ⚽⚽⚽ ⚽⚽ 👟

....

⚽👟 ⚽👟⚽⚽ ⚽👟👟 ⚽👟 👟⚽👟👟 ⚽⚽⚽

....

⚽👟⚽⚽ ⚽ ⚽⚽👟⚽ 👟

....

👟 👟👟👟 👟👟⚽ 👟 👟👟👟

....

👟 ⚽⚽ 👟⚽⚽ 👟⚽👟👟 ⚽⚽👟 ⚽👟👟⚽

....

64. ON THE FLY

How can you get the ball in the net just by moving your head and the book?

Tip: try looking at the fly.

65. BIBS AND SOCKS

The kit room has a box of bibs containing 20 red bibs and 20 green bibs. The kit room also has a box of socks containing 40 red and 40 green socks. Ben goes into the kit room to fetch some bibs and socks. He discovers the light isn't working. So when he takes a bib from the bib box or a sock from the sock box he has no idea what colour it is.

a) How many bibs does he need to take from the bib box to make sure he has two bibs of different colours?

   The answer is: ....

b) How many socks does he need to take from the sock box to make sure he has a pair in the same colour?

   The answer is: ....

c) How many socks and bibs does he need to take to make sure he has a red bib and a pair of red socks, and a green bib and a pair of green socks?

   The answer is: ....

Look at the word list below. Can you work out why each word has the value given to it? Once you have discovered the rule, fill in the value for GAME.

Word	Value
Hit	0
Kit	0
Net	1
Man	1
Woman	2
Foot	2
Goal	2
Penalty	3
Ball	3
Boot	4
Goooal!	4
Game	

Tip: don't think about the length of the words, or the meaning of the words, but instead the shape of the words.

67. THE NAME GAME

Otto, Ada, Pip, Bob and Eve play for Palindrome FC. They are looking for new players. Which of the following names are they most likely to choose?

Harry
Hannah
Robbie
Megan
Neymar

The answer is: ....

Harry   Hannah   Robbie   Megan   Neymar

68. LATIN CLASS

Rovers have just signed three South Americans: Juan, Pedro and Chico. They come from three different countries and play in three different positions: defence, midfield and attack. Can you work out which player in which position plays for which country?

Juan isn't from Chile.
The midfielder is a distant cousin of the Peruvian, who's called Chico.
The striker is from Paraguay.

You might find it helpful to fill in this chart.

	Chile	Peru	Paraguay
Juan			
Pedro			
Chico			
Defender			
Midfielder			
Striker			

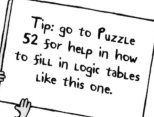

Tip: go to Puzzle 52 for help in how to fill in logic tables like this one.

Can you discover what links these four images?

a)

b)

c)

d)

The answer is: ....

Six shirts are laid out in the pattern below:

This pattern is called a **number sandwich** because:

A single shirt is sandwiched between the 1s.
Two shirts are sandwiched between the 2s.
Three shirts are sandwiched between the 3s.

On this page, we want you to create a number sandwich with the following eight shirts, which have two instances each of 1, 2, 3 and 4:

In this number sandwich, one shirt must be sandwiched between the 1s, two shirts between the 2s, three shirts between the 3s and four shirts between the 4s. Once you have found an arrangement that works, draw the numbers in the shirts below.

Tip: you might find this easiest to solve if you cut out the eight digits on a piece of paper and rearrange them.

71. ALPHABET SOUP

Georgia is a country of 4 million people at the far eastern border of Europe. Georgia does not use the Roman alphabet, but instead its own alphabet. Here is how you write the names of four British cities in Georgian. Each letter in Georgian corresponds to a letter (or in rare cases two letters) in our alphabet.

ბ რ ი ს ტ ო ლ ი
B R I S T O L I

ლ ი ვ ე რ პ უ ლ ი
L I V E R P O O L I

ლ ო ნ დ ო ნ ი
L O N D O N I

მ ა ნ ჩ ე ს ტ ე რ ი
M A N CH E S T E R I

> Tip: in Georgian, these cities are pronounced with an 'i' at the end. You can ignore that letter. If the English spelling seems funny, read it aloud to get the answer!

Can you fill in the missing British cities below?

ბ ი რ მ ი ნ გ ე მ ი
. . . . I

ლ ე ს ტ ე რ ი
. I

ნ ო ტ ი ნ გ ე მ ი
. . . . I

88

72. BOOT CAMP

Fill in the following word ladders. For some, we've given you an extra clue.

a)

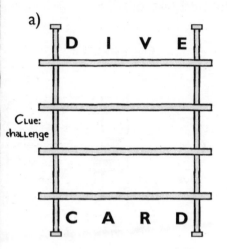

D I V E

Clue: challenge

C A R D

b)

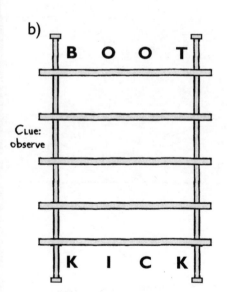

B O O T

Clue: observe

K I C K

c)

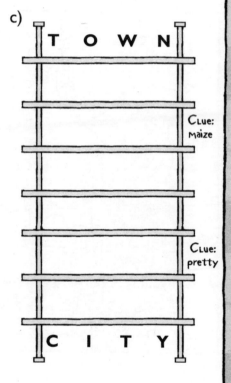

T O W N

Clue: maize

Clue: pretty

C I T Y

Tip: see Puzzle 5 for word ladder rules.

Something's gone wrong in the football factory!

Can you spot the ball that is the odd one out?

5cm

Pinocchio's nose

Pinocchio's nose is 5cm long. He is standing on the goal line of a football pitch which is 100m from end to end, facing the opposing goal.

When Pinocchio lies his nose doubles in length. When he lies a second time, it doubles in length again, and it continues to double in length with each lie after that. After how many lies does his nose poke into the opposition net?

Pinocchio's position on the goal-line

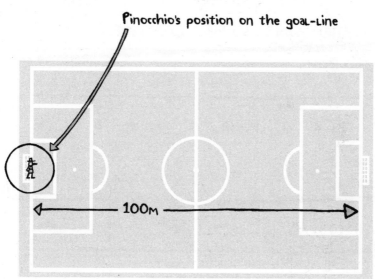

100M

The answer is: ....

75. A MISSING VOWEL

On each of the scoreboards below is a scoreline with the vowels taken out. For each scoreboard, the original scoreline only used one vowel, although this vowel was used several times. Can you work out which vowel is missing from each of the scoreboards, and find the teams and scores?

Here is an example:

B L T N   T W   M K   D N S   T W

Vowel is: O
Score is: BOLTON TWO MK DONS TWO

a)

X T R   T H R L D S   S V N

Vowel is:
Score is:

b)

P S W C H   S X   G R M S B Y   N L

Vowel is:
Score is:

92

a) A famous old footballer had great grandchildren, yet none of his grandchildren had any children. How is this possible?

The answer is: ....

b) What do dead people eat, but if living people eat it they die?

The answer is: ....

77. WHERE'S THE BALL?

Find the 30 balls hidden in the picture along with Ben, Alex, Spike and Pickles the dog.

78. FOLLOW THE BALL

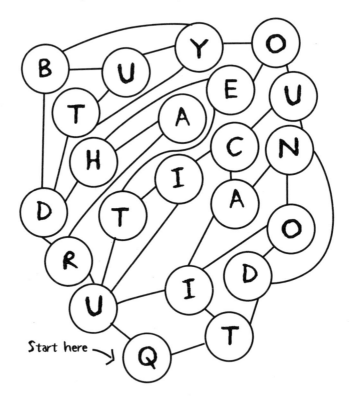

The image below shows 22 positions of a ball as it moves around a pitch, joined by lines. The correct path of the ball starts at Q and then, moving only along the lines, passes through all the other letters, spelling out a phrase of seven English words. The path passes each letter once and only once. Can you discover the phrase?

The answer is quite hard but you can do it!

Start here →

The answer is: ....

Tip: don't go back on yourself! Each letter that you pass through is used only once.

Below is a Venn diagram about different sports. Can you think of eight sports to place in the positions 1 to 8?

Here's a start: position 5 must be a team sport that uses a round ball and involves kicking. Does anything come to mind? Some of the positions have many possible answers. Try to come up with as many examples for each of the positions as possible.

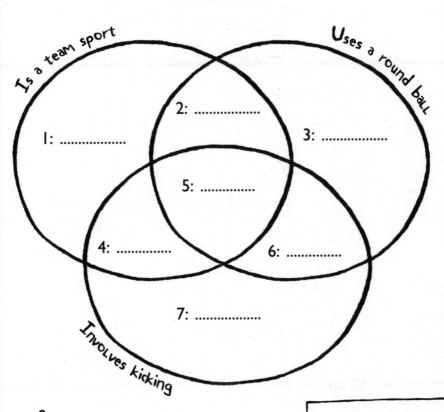

Is a team sport

Uses a round ball

Involves kicking

1: ....

2: ....

3: ....

4: ....

5: ....

6: ....

7: ....

8: ....

Tip: if you've forgotten what a Venn diagram is, it's explained in Puzzle 35.

When a national team wins the World Cup, it is customary for them to add a star to the team badge. That's why Brazil has five stars on their badge – they have won the World Cup five times. There is a star in the picture below. Can you find it?

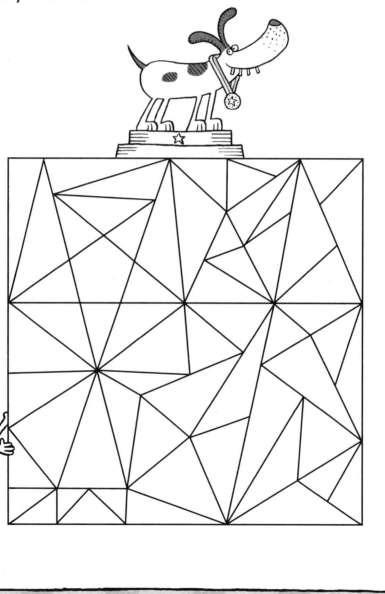

In each of the additions below, each symbol stands for a different digit. Can you work out what digit each symbol is, in order for the addition to make sense?

a)

+ ⚽

_____

🧤 ⚽

⚽ is........

〰 is........

b)

+

_____

🄲 is........

👟 is........

🧤 is........

Can you find anagrams of the following phrases? An anagram is when you rearrange the letters to make a new word or phrase. Here the anagrams are all famous European football clubs.

a)

The answer is: ....

b)

The answer is: ....

c)

M O N K E Y   D I V A

The answer is: ....

d)

R E A L   B A C O N

The answer is: ....

e)

U R B A N   C H I M N E Y

The answer is: ....

Here's a conversation that happened between four players of the same team:

> Striker: I scored the goal.
> Midfielder: The striker is lying.
> Defender: The midfielder is lying.
> Goalkeeper: The defender is lying.

How many of the footballers are telling the truth?

Here's one way to tackle the problem. First, assume the striker is telling the truth. From this information, deduce one by one which of his team-mates are lying and which are telling the truth. Next, assume the striker is lying, and go through the players one by one once again.

The answer is: ....

....

84. SILLY SIGNS

Simon the sign painter painted some signs at Football School, but he painted exactly one letter wrong in each word. Can you work out which letters are wrong in each of these signs? Write the correct words in the spaces below. We've done the first one for you.

a) SOADIUM

...**STADIUM**...

b) TOBLET

....

c) ERTER

....

d) QUIST

....

e) ELIT

....

f) WAG TUT

....

g) GO FUNNING

....

h) STORY BOOM

....

85. AROUND THE WORLD

Can you guess which country is represented in each picture?

a)

....

b)

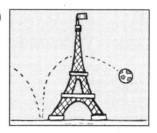

....

c)

....

d)

....

1. Megan Rapinoe is from

....

2. Kylian Mbappé is from

....

3. Harry Kane is from

....

4. Neymar is from

....

86. MISSING NATIONS

[A₁]

Find the countries below – who have all been to a World Cup – in the grid.

A	S	U	B	U	L	G	A	R	I	A	S	C
M	T	N	E	W	Z	E	A	L	A	N	D	E
A	A	O	L	O	S	D	E	C	C	C	N	L
N	N	C	G	H	A	N	A	H	U	R	A	S
A	I	I	I	O	X	A	I	B	N	I	L	A
P	T	R	U	F	Y	L	A	T	I	A	R	L
Y	N	A	M	R	E	G	M	N	G	P	E	V
A	E	N	I	I	A	N	R	U	T	G	H	A
U	G	K	U	V	E	E	T	E	Y	E	T	D
G	R	O	R	D	I	R	D	P	E	A	E	O
U	A	S	E	U	O	L	T	A	S	C	N	R
R	S	W	P	P	T	N	O	W	A	L	E	S
U	S	I	R	A	Q	A	I	B	R	E	S	L

Argentina	El Salvador	Italy	Sweden
Belgium	England	Netherlands	Togo
Bolivia	Germany	New Zealand	Turkey
Bulgaria	Ghana	Panama	Uruguay
Chile	Greece	Peru	USA
Cuba	Iran	Portugal	USSR
Egypt	Iraq	Serbia	Wales

Once you have crossed out all these countries you will have 25 letters left in the grid. Rearrange them to make four other countries who have also been to the World Cup.

The answer is: ....

Tip: two are World Cup winners, one is in the Americas and the other is closer to home!

Ben needs to water the pitch at Football School. Which of these two watering cans can carry the most water?

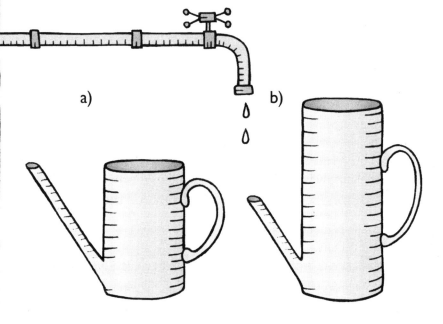

a)   b)

The answer is: ....

88. WHO OWNS THE CAT

Four football fans from different countries are attending a World Cup. They each have a different pet, support a different Premier League team, and were born in a different month.

The Wolves fan was born on Christmas Day.
The Australian was born in February.
The Canadian's dog is called Candy.
The hamster owner has the last birthday of the year.
The person with the earliest birthday in the year supports Arsenal and doesn't have the goldfish.
The Newcastle fan was born on Halloween.
The Bolivian has a birthday a month after the Australian.

Use the statements above to work out:
Who does the Dane support? Who supports Liverpool?
Who has a pet cat? You might find it helpful to fill in this chart.

Nationality	Team	Pet	Month
Australian			
Bolivian			
Canadian			
Dane			

The Dane supports ....

The Liverpool supporter is ....

The cat belongs to the ....

Ben has a set of football cards. All of the cards have a player on one side and the name of a country on the other. There are cards with men on them, and cards with women.

Alex takes four of the cards and places them on the table as above. Two have the country face up and two have players face up.
Alex says of these four cards: "If a card has England on one side, it has a male player on the other."

Which cards do you need to turn over to prove what Alex says is true?

The answer is: ....

The Peterborough United mascot is a rabbit called Peter Burrows. Here are three Peters and three ears.

Can you complete the image below so that there are three Peters and three ears drawn in such a way that each Peter has two ears?

Across:

2. Ham and Bromwich Albion (4)
5. You might say this when you get hurt (4)
6. Dele .... (4)
8. Where you take the penalty from (4)
9. These can be either left or right (4)
10. If the ball crosses this, it's a goal (4)
11. Party food (4)
13. An attempt at goal (4)
16. When you pretend to have been fouled (4)
17. On the .... of the box (4)

Down:

1. The bit just before you kick a penalty (3-2)
2. Peep peep! (7)
3. A good defender will make a lot of these (7)
4. Bright, shiny earrings, necklaces, rings and other jewellery (5)
11. Red or yellow? (4)
12. Capital city whose main team is called Dynamo (4)
14. The .... of God (4)
15. Extra .... (4)

92. EURO HEROES

The word for France in French is France. But the word for Germany in German is not Germany – it's Deutschland. Can you work out what the following European countries are called in English? Each one is written in the language of that country. Write your answers in the spaces below.

a) ESPAÑA

....

b) HELLAS

....

c) HRVATSKA

....

d) ÍSLAND

....

e) MAGYARORSZÁG

....

f) NEDERLAND

....

g) NORGE

....

h) ÖSTERREICH

....

i) POLSKA

....

j) SHQIPËRIA

....

k) SUOMI

....

l) EESTI

....

Tip: some of them contain similarities to the English names, but for the others just have a guess!

Which football scarf is bigger?

a)

b)

The answer is: ....

94. SMUDGED TABLE

Ben dropped his drink on the World Cup group table below and some of the numbers got smudged out. Can you fill in the table and work out what the scores of all the games were?

Teams are only allowed to play each other once, but maybe not all the matches have been played.
You will need to make lots of deductions. One thing to realize, for example, is that the sum of all the won games must equal the sum of all the lost games, because every time a team wins a game, another team loses a game.

	Matches played	Won	Lost	Drawn	Goals scored	Goals conceded	Points
Algeria	3	2			5	5	
Bolivia		1		0	2	0	
Croatia				0	1	1	
Denmark							

How many words can you make using **only** the letters:

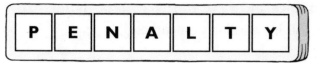

That's one P, one E, one N, one A, one L, one T and one Y.
If you play, and don't nap, you'll find there are plenty!

a) Two-letter words:

A	N

b) Three-letter words. We found at least 20:

N	A	P

c) Four-letter words:

P	L	A	Y

d) Five-letter words:

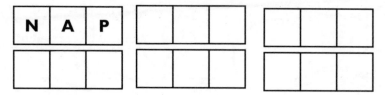

P	A	N	E	L

e) Six-letter words:

Tip: see Puzzle
53 if you forgot
how to do
this puzzle.

Can you find your way through the football funfair? Start at the entrance and make your way through the maze to the exit. If you hit a ball, it's a dead end!

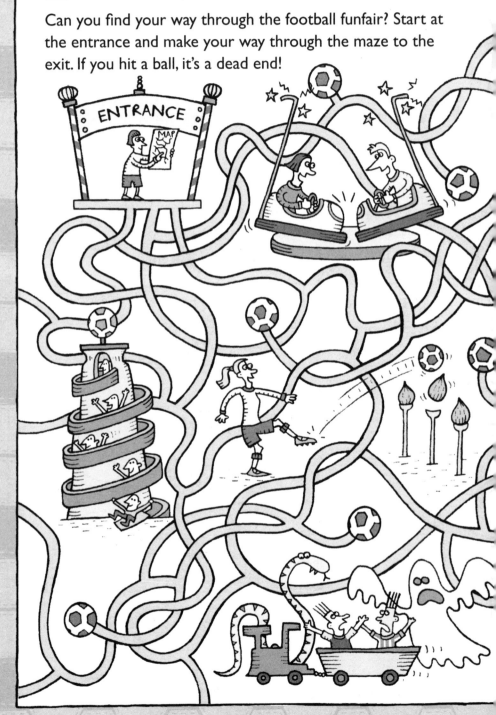

116

At half-time, Alex lines up six tumblers of juice for the team. The tumblers are full and empty in alternate order, as below:

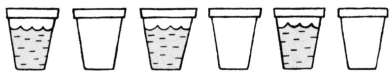

Ben arrives and he rearranges the line so that the three tumblers on the left are full, and the three tumblers on the right are empty. He manages to do this, however, by moving only one of the tumblers. What did he do?

The answer is: ....

98. SILLY SENTENCES

We've hidden a British football club in each of the following sentences. Can you spot them all?

a) Alex put the ice-cream tub right on the table.

The answer is: ....

b) Ben knows never to never say never.

The answer is: ....

c) I owe St Hamish a prayer.

The answer is: ....

d) He didn't say much else apart from "Hi".

The answer is: ....

e) In the parcel: tickets!

The answer is: ....

f) She tries to keep her cool.

The answer is: ....

Tip: for help in answering this problem, see Puzzle 62.

a) What do the British club Reading FC and the French club OGC Nice have in common?

The answer is: ....

b) An old and a young footballer were chatting at the training ground. The young footballer was the son of the old footballer, but the old footballer was not the father of the young footballer. How come?

The answer is: ....

100. GIVE AND TAKE

In this dot-to-dot puzzle, join the numbers by adding 7s and subtracting 4s. Start at 1. Add 7 and join to that number. Then subtract 4 and join to that next number. Add 7. Join to that number. Subtract 4. Join to that number. Continue in this way until you fill all the dots you can. What picture do you make?

You might find it helpful to write out the sequence of numbers before you join the dots.

Tip: the first numbers are 1, 8, 4.

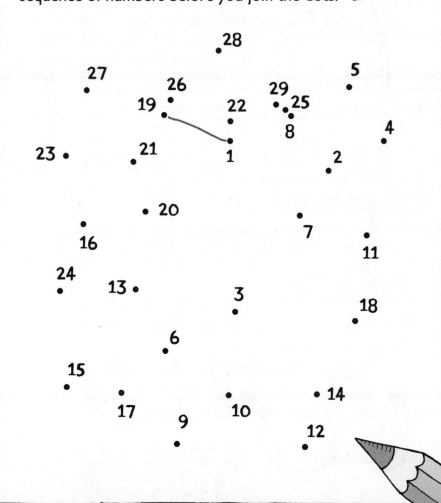

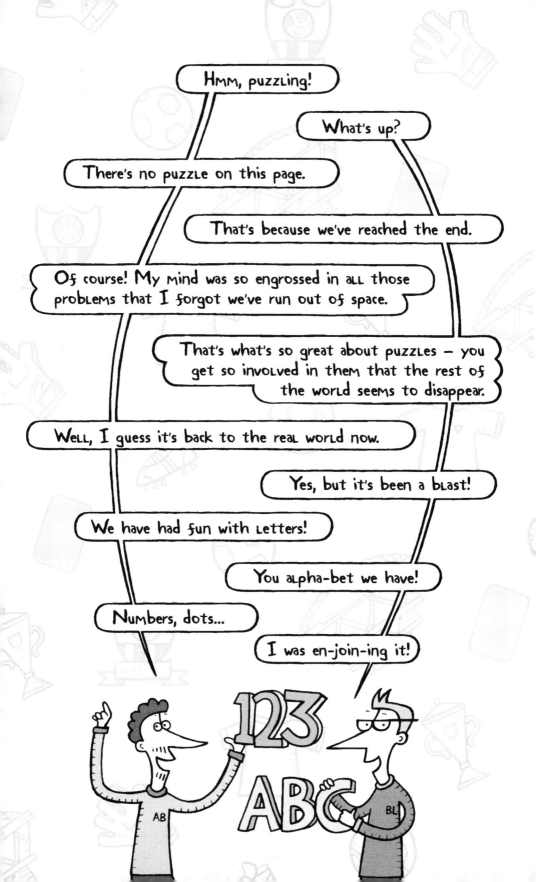

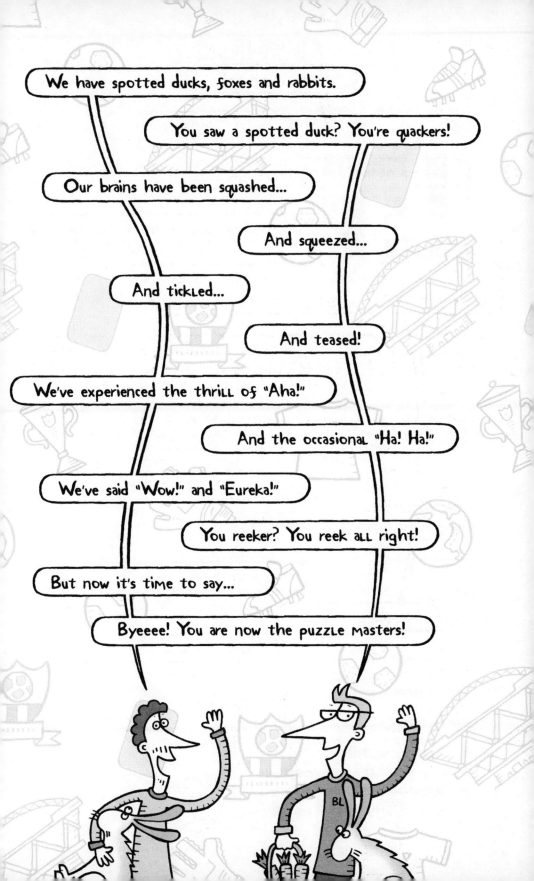

ANSWERS

1. Rotate the duck by 90 degrees and you will see a rabbit.

2.

¹·E	V	²·E	R	T	O	N
G		A				
Y		³·G	⁴·O	A	L	⁵·S
P		L	S			K
⁶·T	R	E	N	T		U
			O			L
⁷·A	R	S	E	N	A	L

3. The number five: five fingers, five-a-side, 5 o'clock, five weekdays.

4. They are two of a set of triplets! They have a brother, Agostino, who also plays for the college football team.

5. a)

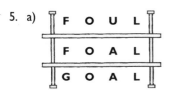

F O U L
F O A L
G O A L

b)

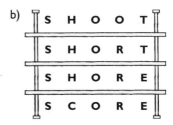

S H O O T
S H O R T
S H O R E
S C O R E

6. is number 4

is number 3

is number 6

is number 2

is number 5

is number 1

is number 8

7. The headline says:

   a) Striker nets hat-**TRICK**
   b) Star in **WORLD**-record transfer bid
   c) Under**DOG** beats Utd in FA Cup shock
   d) My penalty **SHOOT-OUT** nightmare

8. Argentina scored 0 points, so they must have lost both their games. They
    didn't score any goals, so we can put 0 as their score to both their games.
    Peru conceded two goals. We know Argentina didn't score these, so Brazil
    must have scored them in their match against Peru. So you can put 2 in
    Brazil's score for Brazil v. Peru.
    Brazil scored 3 goals. We know 2 of these were against Peru. So the third
    goal must have been in their other match against Argentina. We can put 1
    in their score.
    We also know Brazil let in 1 goal. It can't have been in their match
    against Argentina, so 1 must be Peru's score against Brazil.
    Peru scored 2 goals in total. So their other goal must be the winning goal
    against Argentina.

Brazil v. Peru	
Brazil	2
Peru	1

Peru v. Argentina	
Peru	1
Argentina	0

Brazil v. Argentina	
Brazil	1
Argentina	0

9.

10. a) and e) will make a knot.

11. a) They are in a stadium taking part in a Mexican wave.
    b) The match was an important game, like a cup final, and the happy players are
        crying tears of joy. The losing players are keeping up appearances in order to
        appear respectful and gracious in defeat.

12. There are many different variations. Here are three!

a) 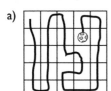 b) c)

13. The trophy is filled with 60 balls.

14.

Position	Team
1.	Rovers
2.	Town
3.	Albion
4.	United
5.	City

15. The answer is 7m.
First, we need to work out the height of the rectangle, which is the same on both sides.
So, if **area = width x height**, then we can work out the height of the left side:
30m² = 5m x height, which is 6m. That means the height of the right side is 6m too.
So now we can work out the missing width. If **42m² = ? x 6m**, then ? must be 7m.

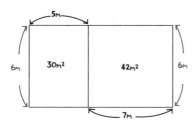

16.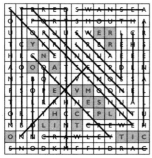

The shaded letters are the ones that aren't in any of the words. And the letters spell
LIVERPOOL and MANCHESTER CITY.

17. The answer is c) because it has 6 sections on the shirt. The first shirt has 1 section, the second has 2, the third 3, the fourth 4, the fifth 5, so the sixth shirt must have 6.

18. a) Second place
    b) The second problem is a trick question – you cannot edge past the team in bottom place, because you cannot be below the team in bottom place!

19. The sixth fan hasn't gone anywhere! What has happened is the pieces of the footballers' heads have been rearranged in such a way to make five heads rather than six. When there are five heads, the heads are on average slightly bigger than when there are six heads, to make up for the missing extra head. Look at it this way: in the first picture, four heads are made from two parts, but two heads (the third one along, and the last one) are made from only one part. In the second picture, all the heads have two parts. What's clever about this puzzle is that even when you know how it is done it still feels like magic to see one of the fans disappear!

20. The missing piece is a).

21. The odd one out is the trophy.
    The football boot is repeated 3 times.

22. a) Megan Rapinoe
    b) Cristiano Ronaldo
    c) Lionel Messi
    d) Gareth Bale

23. a) The plane has already landed and is parked on the tarmac. The players see the mountain range from the window.
    b) In summer in Tromsø, the sun never sets! Tromsø IL are based in the city of Tromsø, which is inside the Arctic Circle, making the club the most northerly top-league club in the world. For about two months in summer, from mid-May to mid-July, the sun never sets. So if Lars went to see the match, say, in mid-May or June, he could easily live in a stadium for a week and get back home before the sun goes down – since it will only go down in mid-July.

24. a) 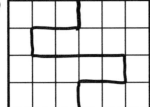 b)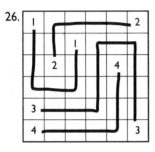

25. b) A Year has 12 Months.
    c) A Match lasts for 90 Minutes.
    d) A Hand has 5 Fingers.
    e) The Premier League has 20 Clubs.

    f) A Day has 24 Hours.
    g) England have won 1 World Cup.
    h) If you score 3 Goals, it's a Hat-Trick.

26.

27.

Player name:	Left peg	Middle peg	Right peg
	Jones	Smith	Robinson
Squad number:	3	7	5
Boot colour:	white	pink	orange

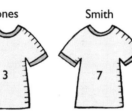

28.

29. Half-time starts at 4.55 p.m.

30. If you turn the page to the side, you will see that the scoreline spells ONION.

31. b)

U	R	U	G	U	A	Y

c)

G	E	R	M	A	N	Y

d)

E	N	G	L	A	N	D

e)

B	R	A	Z	I	L

f)

F	R	A	N	C	E

g)

A	R	G	E	N	T	I	N	A

h)

I	T	A	L	Y

32. a) Manchester United   d) Aston Villa
    b) Wigan Athletic   e) Stoke City
    c) Tottenham Hotspur   f) Leicester City

33. The match was on Tuesday.

34. It's the Premier League trophy!

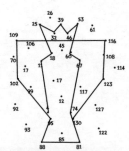

35. The answers are: 1. Bernardo Silva, 2. Mo Salah, 3. John Stones, 4. Raheem Sterling, 5. Harry Kane and 6. Harry Maguire.

36. The words socks, box, fox and clocks all rhyme.

37. The answer is £5 million and £105 million.

38. Hull and Millwall. You can read the words if you read the page at an angle.

39.

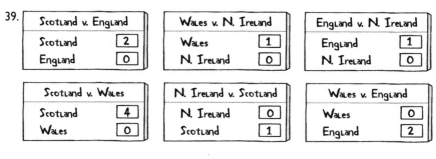

Scotland v. England			Wales v. N. Ireland			England v. N. Ireland	
Scotland	2		Wales	1		England	1
England	0		N. Ireland	0		N. Ireland	0

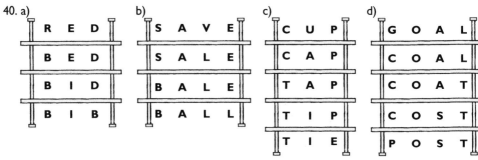

Scotland v. Wales			N. Ireland v. Scotland			Wales v. England	
Scotland	4		N. Ireland	0		Wales	0
Wales	0		Scotland	1		England	2

40. a)

R	E	D
B	E	D
B	I	D
B	I	B

b)

S	A	V	E
S	A	L	E
B	A	L	E
B	A	L	L

c)

C	U	P
C	A	P
T	A	P
T	I	P
T	I	E

d)

G	O	A	L
C	O	A	L
C	O	A	T
C	O	S	T
P	O	S	T

41. Baby
Backpack
Badger
Bag
Bagpipes
Bales of hay
Ball
Ballet dancer
Balloon (hot air)
Balloon (small)
Bandage on Alex
Barking dog
Barn
Bat
Bear
Beard
Beaver
Bed
Beehive
Beekeeper
Bees
Bell
Belltower
Belt
Ben
Bench
Bib

Bike
Billygoat
Biplane
Bird(s)
Birdbox
Biscuit
Blanket
Boat
Bodybuilder

Bogroll
Bolts (in box)
Bones (in box)
Boots
Bottles
Box
Boy
Bricks
Broom

Brush
Bucket
Budgie
Buggy (for baby)
Bugle
Buildings
Bulb
Bunny rabbit
Bush

42. a) 4
    b) 6
    c) 10
    d) 2
    e) 3

43. From left to right: goalkeeping coach, physio, assistant coach, coach.

44. is number 2

 is number 4

 is number 10

 is number 3

(flag icon) is number 1

 is number 6

 is number 9

 is number 7

 is number 5

(shirt icon) is number 8

45. BOX. It is the only word that consists of letters that are the same when reflected horizontally. (Imagine there was a horizontal line through the middle of these letters. If you put a mirror on that line, either facing up, or facing down, the letter would still look the same because the top half and the bottom half of the letter are the same.)

46.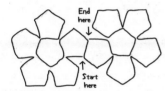

47. The answer is d). If Christie is to the right of Amber, then Amber must be to the left of Christie. We know that Amber is also to the left of Beth. This means Amber is to the left of both Beth and Christie, which means she must be furthest to the left.

48. The message is: OUR OPPONENTS ARE A GOOD TEAM BUT WE CAN BEAT THEM IF WE CROWD THE GOALKEEPER AT CORNERS BECAUSE HE IS NOT CONFIDENT AT HIGH BALLS AND IF WE PLAY THE BALL DOWN THE SIDE OF THE LEFT BACK AS SHE IS SLOWER THAN OUR WINGER

49. The answer is $16m^2$. Following the same rule as Puzzle 15, we first need to work out the width of the first square on the left. So, if **area = width x height, $9m^2$ = width x 3m**, which is 3m. We now need to work out the width of the rectangle. We know the first square width is 3m, and the total width of the first square and rectangle is 6m, so **6m - 3m = rectangle width**, which is 3m. We now need to work out the height of the rectangle, following the same rule, **$21m^2$ = 3m x height**, which is 7m. We can now work out the height and width of the square on the right. We know the rectangle width is 3m, and the total width of the second square and rectangle is 7m, so **7m - 3m = 4m**. We also know the height of the rectangle is 7m. We can see that the height of the two squares is equal to the height of the rectangle. So the height of the second square must be **7m - 3m = 4m**. Therefore, **area = 4m x 4m**, which is $16m^2$.

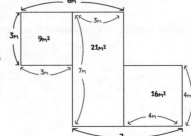

50.

¹A	²C H	E	³S		⁴G
R	E	M			A
⁵R	A N	G	E	R	S
O			L		
⁶W	E	⁷M	B	L E	⁸Y
		R			E
		⁹S	P	U R	S

51. Los Angeles: 9 a.m.
Sydney: 4 a.m.
Tokyo: 1.45 a.m.
New Delhi: 3.45 a.m.
Manchester: 7.30 a.m.

52.

	Celtic	Swansea	Everton	Chicken	Cucumber	Cheese
Mo	x	✓	x	x	x	✓
Jo	✓	x	x	✓	x	x
Flo	x	x	✓	x	✓	x

Which means Mo supports Swansea and eats a cheese sandwich, Jo supports Celtic and eats a chicken sandwich and Flo supports Everton and eats a cucumber sandwich.

53. Two-letter words: AT, TO, TA, LO, FA, LA, OF.
Three-letter words: ALL, BAT, BOO, FAB, FAT, FOB, LAB, LOB, LOO, LOT, OAF, OAT, TAB, TOO.
Four-letter words: BALL, BLOT, BOAT, BOLT, BOOT, FALL, FLAB, FLAT, FOAL, FOOL, FOOT, LOAF, LOFT, LOOT, TALL, TOLL, TOOL.
Five-letter words: AFOOT, ALOFT, ALOOF, BLOAT, FLOAT, TABOO.

54.

55. Winnie was holding the bucket underwater.

56. The answer is 912.
    From the first two lines we can eliminate the possibility that the digits 0, 3, 4, 6, 7 are in the code. We can deduce from the third line that 9 is one of the correct digits, since we have eliminated 0 and 6. If 9 is one of the correct digits, we can deduce from the fifth line that both 5 and 8 are not in the code. We can also deduce that 9 must be in the first position of the code, since line three tells us it cannot be in the second position and line five tells us it cannot be in the third position. From line four we can deduce that the 1 must be in the code and it must be in the second position. The only digit left is 2, which must be in the third position.

57. a) Timmy Twinkletoes, Lucky Stryker, Beau Peep-Peep
    b) Beau Peep-Peep
    c) Sam Speed: he scored an average of 2 goals a match.
    d) Brad Spitt: he scored on average 1 goal every 10 minutes.

58.

59.

60.

Bayern v. Barcelona	
Bayern	3
Barcelona	0

PSG v. Juventus	
PSG	0
Juventus	2

Bayern v. Juventus	
Bayern	2
Juventus	1

Barcelona v. PSG	
Barcelona	2
PSG	0

PSG v. Bayern	
PSG	0
Bayern	2

Juventus v. Barcelona	
Juventus	0
Barcelona	0

First, let's work out how many matches each team won, drew or lost. Bayern Munich have 9 points, so they must have won all three matches. Juventus and Barcelona have 4 points, so they must have won one and drawn one. Since PSG have 0 points, they lost every game. This must mean that Juventus and Barcelona drew the match they played together.

If Bayern beat Barcelona 3-0, and we know that Barcelona only conceded 3 goals in all three matches, then Barcelona must have conceded no other goals. So in their other games their opposition scored 0. Since we know they drew against Juventus, that game must have been 0-0. Barcelona's 2 goals must, therefore, have come against PSG. PSG scored no goals at all, so we can add this score to all their games. Since neither Barcelona nor PSG scored against Bayern, their I goal against must have been scored by Juventus. And since Juventus scored 3 in total, they must have scored 2 against PSG. Juventus conceded 2 goals, and these must have been scored by Bayern. Bayern scored 7 in all, so they must have got 2 past PSG.

61. The clue tells us that the most common letter in the original message is "E". The most common letter in the coded message is "H". Since H is 3 letters after E in the alphabet (EFGH), the shift must be 3.
The message says:
DON'T TELL BEN BUT I HID THE CAKE IN THE LIBRARY. I'LL MEET YOU THERE AS SOON AS THE GAME STARTS.

62. b) Ajax
   c) Napoli
   d) Porto
   e) Real Madrid

63. The message is: WHY IS IT ALWAYS LEFT TO ME TO TIDY UP

64. Stare at the fly, and then move the page towards you until it touches your nose. You will see the ball shoot into the goal!

65. The answers are a) 21 bibs, b) 41 socks, c) 21 bibs and 42 socks.

66. **Game** = 2. That's because the numbers are counting the number of loops in the letter. The letters a, o, e and P have a single loop, and B has two loops. All the other letters have no loops.

67. Hannah. A palindrome is a word that is the same when spelled forwards and backwards. Everyone in Palindrome FC has a name that is a palindrome.

68. Juan is a striker from Paraguay, Pedro is a midfielder from Chile and Chico is a defender from Peru.

	Chile	Peru	Paraguay
Juan	x	x	✓
Pedro	✓	x	x
Chico	x	✓	x
Defender	x	✓	x
Midfielder	✓	x	x
Striker	x	x	✓

69. Each picture shows a different meaning of the word cross: crossing the ball, a Christian cross, a cross person, and a chicken crossing the road.

70. The answer is:

or backwards:

71. From looking at Liverpool and London, which both start with a ლ, you can deduce that this letter is an 'L'. Looking at the repeated letters in London, you can work out that the 'o' and 'n' must be 'ო' and 'ნ'. Gradually the words begin to make sense. You may have spotted that all the Georgian words end with a 'o', which is the 'i' sound. This is because Georgian pronunciation adds an 'i' to the ends of words that end in a consonant. Hope you weren't too confused!

British cities	Georgian translation
Bristol	ბრისტოლი
Liverpool	ლივერპული
London	ლონდონი
Manchester	მანჩესტერი
Birmingham	ბირმინგები
Leicester	ლესტერი
Nottingham	ნოტინგები

72. a) b) c)

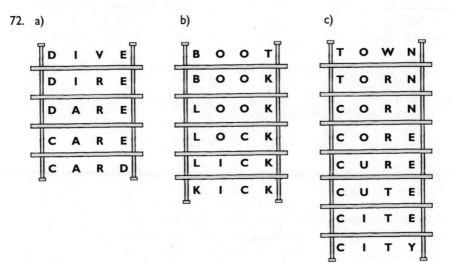

73.

74. After 11 lies, when his nose will be 102.4m long

75. a) Vowel is 'E'. Score is EXETER THREE LEEDS SEVEN.
    b) Vowel is 'I'. Score is IPSWICH SIX GRIMSBY NIL.

76. a) Because his grandchildren were great people!
    b) Nothing.

77.

78. The answer is QUITE HARD BUT YOU CAN DO IT – just like it said in the question!

79. The answers have several examples for some of the positions: 1. ice hockey, curling, bobsleigh, 2. basketball, handball, volleyball, cricket, 3. golf, singles tennis, 4. rugby, American football, 5. football, 6. freestyle football, 7. kickboxing, 8. running.

80.

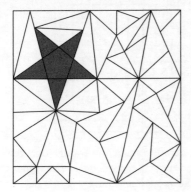

81. a) is 5

 is 1

b) is 0

 is 1

 is 9

82. a) Real Madrid   d) Barcelona
    b) Benfica   e) Bayern Munich
    c) Dynamo Kiev

83. Two are telling the truth. (If the striker is telling the truth, the midfielder is lying, which means that the defender is telling the truth, which means the goalkeeper is lying. If the striker is not telling the truth, however, then the midfielder is telling the truth, the defender is lying and the keeper is telling the truth. Either way, two people are telling the truth, although we don't know which two.)

84. b) Toilet   f) Way Out
    c) Enter   g) No Running
    d) Quiet   h) Store Room
    e) Exit

85. a) England
    b) France
    c) Brazil
    d) USA

    1. d)
    2. b)
    3. a)
    4. c)

137

86. The shaded letters are the ones that are not in any of the words. They can be rearranged to make France, Spain, Mexico, Scotland.

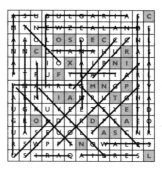

87. The shorter watering can on the left, marked a), will contain more water than the higher watering can on the right. The water level in a watering can will never rise higher than the height of its spout, since water will leak out the spout if any more water is put in. You will, therefore, be able to fill the left watering can to the brim, which is higher than the level of the spout of the watering can on the right.

88. Here's how to solve it: the Canadian has a dog called Candy, and the Australian was born in February, so they can both go in the grid.

Nationality	Team	Pet	Month
Australian			February
Bolivian			
Canadian		dog	
Dane			

If the Bolivian has a birthday a month after the Australian, that month must be March. The questions tell us someone was born on Christmas Day, and someone on Halloween. This means the earliest birthday in the year is February. So, as the person with the earliest birthday in the year supports Arsenal, the Australian must support Arsenal. This information can go in too.

Nationality	Team	Pet	Month
Australian	Arsenal		February
Bolivian			March
Canadian		dog	
Dane			

The last birthday of the year is Christmas Day. So the person born in December is either the Canadian or the Dane. But the person born in December has a hamster, so that person cannot be the Canadian, who has a dog. It must be the Dane. The Canadian must, therefore, be the person born on Halloween.

Nationality	Team	Pet	Month
Australian	Arsenal		February
Bolivian			March
Canadian		dog	October
Dane		hamster	December

The Newcastle fan was born on Halloween, so the Canadian is a Newcastle fan, and the Wolves fan was born on Christmas Day, so the Dane is a Wolves fan. The Arsenal supporter doesn't have the goldfish, so the Bolivian must have the goldfish.

Nationality	Team	Pet	Month
Australian	Arsenal		February
Bolivian		goldfish	March
Canadian	Newcastle	dog	October
Dane	Wolves	hamster	December

From the question, we know that one of the people has a pet cat and one supports Liverpool. So we can fill these answers in the only boxes left. In conclusion, the Dane supports Wolves, the Liverpool supporter is Bolivian and the cat belongs to the Australian.

Nationality	Team	Pet	Month
Australian	Arsenal	cat	February
Bolivian	Liverpool	goldfish	March
Canadian	Newcastle	dog	October
Dane	Wolves	hamster	December

89. You need to turn over the first and the fourth cards.

You need to turn over the first card to check that it has a man on the other side.
You don't need to turn over the second card, since it does not matter what is on the back of Scotland cards.

You don't need to turn over the third card either, since if it says England, then it is true that England cards have a man on the back, but if it says Scotland then it doesn't matter what is on the back, since Alex's statement is only about cards with England on.
You do need to turn over the fourth card. If it says England on the other side, then it is a card with England on one side and a woman on the other, which means that Alex's statement is false. So in order to make sure Alex's statement is true, we need to turn this card over to make sure it does not say England on it.

90.

91.

	R	W	E	S	T		B	
O	U	C	H		A	L	L	I
	N		I		C		I	
	U		S		K		N	
S	P	O	T		L	E	G	S
		L	I	N	E			
C	A	K	E		S	H	O	T
A		I			H		I	
R		E			A		M	
D	I	V	E		E	D	G	E

92. a) Spain
    b) Greece
    c) Croatia
    d) Iceland
    e) Hungary
    f) Netherlands
    g) Norway
    h) Austria
    i) Poland
    j) Albania
    k) Finland
    l) Estonia

93. You probably thought that the bottom scarf is bigger. In fact, they are both the same size. This puzzle is an optical illusion – our eyes trick us!

94.

	Matches played	Won	Lost	Drawn	Goals scored	Goals conceded	Points
Algeria	3	2	1	0	5	5	6
Bolivia	1	1	0	0	2	0	3
Croatia	2	1	1	0	1	1	3
Denmark	2	0	2	0	3	5	0

Here's how we get there: Algeria played 3 and won 2. Their other game must have been a defeat, since if it was a draw, they would not have equal goals scored and conceded. So we can put a 1 in the Lost column, a 0 in the Drawn column, and 6 in the Points column. If three of the teams have a 0 in the Drawn column, the fourth must have a 0, since if that team played a draw, one of the other teams would have been involved! But we know they didn't since all the others had no drawn matches.

Bolivia conceded no goals, so cannot have lost any games. So put a 0 in the Lost column, a 1 in the Matches played column and a 3 in the Points column. Croatia did not draw, but they scored one goal and conceded one goal. So they must have won one game 1-0 and lost a game 1-0. We can put a 1 in both the Won and the Lost columns, a 2 in the Matches played column and a 3 in the Points column.

So far we know that Algeria played 3, Bolivia played 1 and Croatia played 2. In other words, Algeria played all the other teams (including Denmark). So Bolivia's game must have been against Algeria. Which means that one of Croatia's two games must have been against Denmark. So Denmark played twice, and we can put a 2 in the Matches played column.

The total of the Won column must equal the total of the Lost column, so Denmark must have lost both their games, and we can put a 0 in the Won, a 2 in the Lost and we can put 0 in the Points column.

The games that took place are Algeria v. Bolivia (0-2), Algeria v. Croatia (1-0), Croatia v. Denmark (1-0) and Algeria v. Denmark, which was 4-3 because the remaining number of goals scored for Algeria is 4, and the remaining number of goals conceded is 3.

We finish Denmark's row with a 3 and a 5.

95. There are lots of words you could make with the letters.
Two-letter words: **AN**, AT, LA, PA, TA.
Three-letter words: ANT, ANY, APE, APT, ATE, EAT, LAP, LAY, LET, **NAP**, NET, PAL, PAN, PEN, PEA, PAY, PET, PLY, TAN, TAP, TEA, TEN, YAP, YEP, YET.
Four-letter words: LANE, LATE, LEAN, LEAP, LENT, LEPT, NEAT, PALE, PANE, PANT, PATE, PEAL, PEAT, PELT, PLAN, **PLAY**, PLEA, TALE, TAPE, TYPE, YELP.
Five-letter words: LEANT, LEAPT, **PANEL**, PETAL, PLANE, PLANT, PLATE, PLEAT.
Six-letter words: NEATLY, PLANET, PLENTY.

96.

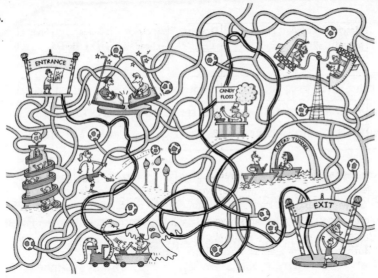

97. Ben picked up the fifth tumbler, poured the juice into the second tumbler, and replaced the empty fifth tumbler in its original position.

98. a) Brighton   c) West Ham   e) Celtic
    b) Everton   d) Chelsea   f) Stoke

99. a) Both clubs are based in cities – Reading and Nice – that also spell words in English. Although, "reading" is pronounced differently from Reading and "nice" is pronounced differently from Nice.
    b) The old footballer was the mother of the young footballer.

100. A shirt!

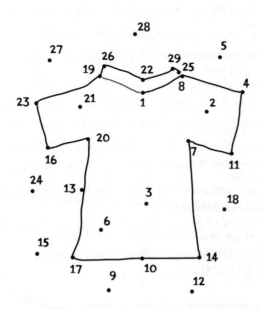

ACKNOWLEDGEMENTS

We have one last puzzle for you: what do you get if you add Alex's love of numbers to Ben's love of football and multiply it by Spike's comical cartooning craft? This book!

The team at Walker stayed logical and level-headed even when their mathematical minds were magnified to the max: head coach Daisy Jellicoe, creative playmaker Laurelie Bazin and sporting director Denise Johnstone-Burt. Thanks also to Ellen Abernethy, Rosi Crawley, Jo Humphreys-Davies, Louise Jackson, Jill Kidson, Megan Middleton, Rebecca Oram and Ed Ripley.

Full marks to our star agents Rebecca Carter, Kirsty Gordon, Ellis Hazelgrove, David Luxton, Rebecca Winfield and Nick Walters.

We would also like to thank the following schools, who tested some of the puzzles in their early stages and provided us with fascinating and friendly feedback. Big shout-outs to the pupils at Stanway School and their teachers Katherine Jones, Susan Jones and Andrea Taylor; and the pupils at Sarum Hall and their teachers Carly-Ann Clarke, Stavros Karrettis, Alice Montiel, Christina Pritchard and Victoria Savage. As the book took shape, we also received helpful comments from these Star Puzzlers: Lucas and Mia Christenson, Billy Kidson, Clemmy and Bibi Lyttleton, Louis and Raf Shields, and Zoe and Jamie Stott.

Ben would like to thank Annie, Clemmy and Bibi for their continued support and inspiration. Alex would like to thank Nat, Zak and Barnaby.

ABOUT YOUR COACHES

Alex Bellos writes for the *Guardian*. He has written several bestselling popular science books and created two mathematical colouring books. He loves puzzles.

Ben Lyttleton is a journalist, broadcaster and football consultant. He has written books about how to score the perfect penalty and what we can learn from football's best managers.

Spike Gerrell grew up loving both playing football and drawing pictures. He now gets to draw for a living. At heart, though, he will always be a central midfielder.

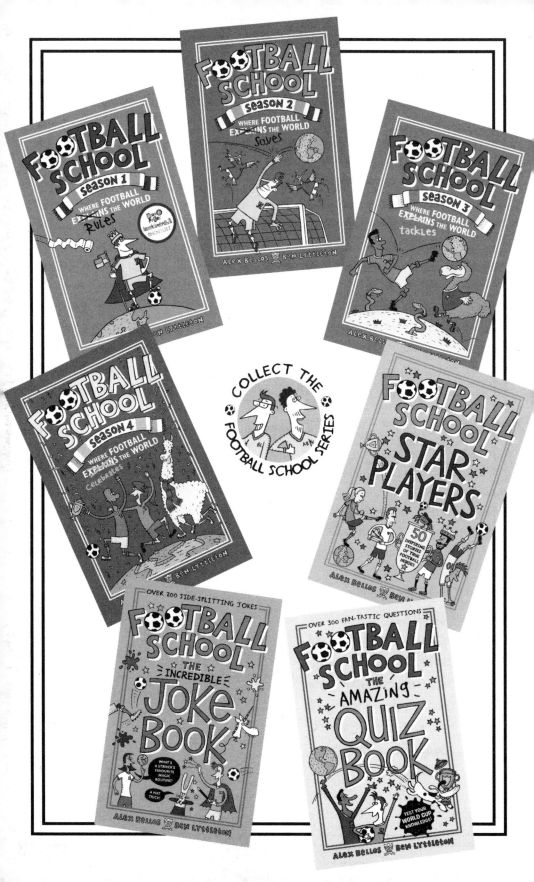